B

By Miriam Frost

Paddles move this boat.

It's a canoe.

Oars move this boat.

It's a rowboat.

Pedals move this boat.

It's a paddleboat.

Sails move this boat.

It's a sailboat.

A motor moves this boat.

It's a motorboat.

A big paddle wheel
moves this boat.

It's a steamboat.

What moves this boat?

A tug boat.